W9-AYF-127

FORCES
AND
MOTION

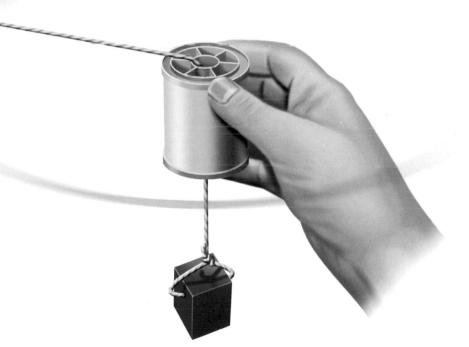

John Graham

KINGFISHER
NEW YORK

KINGFISHER
LONDON & NEW YORK

Distributed in the U.S. and Canada by Macmillan, 175 Fifth Ave., New York, NY 10010

Created for Kingfisher by The Book Makers Ltd
Illustrations: Peter Bull Art Studio

Library of Congress Cataloging-in-Publication data has been applied for.

ISBN: 978-0-7534-6972-9

Kingfisher books are available for special promotions and premiums. For details contact: Special Markets Department, Macmillan, 175 Fifth Ave., New York, NY 10010.

For more information, please visit www.kingfisherbooks.com

Printed in China
9 8 7
7TR/0616/WKT/UG/128MA

Note to readers:
The website addresses listed in this book are correct at the time of going to print. However, due to the ever-changing nature of the Internet, website addresses and content can change. Websites can contain links that are unsuitable for children. The publisher cannot be held responsible for changes in website addresses or content, or for information obtained through a third party. We strongly advise that Internet searches be supervised by an adult.

Cover credits: tl Alamy/Paul Doyle; tc Shutterstock/Beth Van Trees; tr Shutterstock/Catalin Petolea; bl Alamy/Janine Weidel; br Shutterstock/Yuri Arcurs

Contents

Getting started

Have you ever wondered why things move the way they do? What makes them start moving? Why do things fall when you drop them? Why is swimming so much harder than walking? You will discover the answers to these questions, and many others, in this book. It is packed full of experiments to try out at home or at school that will help you understand forces and motion.

Feel the force

Every time you ride a bike, turn a door handle, or even just move your arm, you are using forces. They are the invisible pushes and pulls that make everything happen.

What you need

You can find most of the things you need for the activities in this book around your house or garage. If you do not happen to have the exact item shown in the picture, you can probably use something similar that will do the same thing. You may find that you can improve on some of the ideas here. Improvization is part of the fun of doing experiments!

Most of the activities use empty containers. Start saving plastic bottles, tubs, and cartons. You never know what will come in handy!

Your experiments are more likely to be successful if you work carefully and tidy up as you go along.

Having problems

☹ If something doesn't work at first, don't give up.

☺ Look through the instructions and illustrations again to see if there's anything you have missed, then try again.

Athletes, dancers, racecar drivers, and builders all need to understand about forces. Every machine, from a playground seesaw to a space shuttle, relies on forces to work. From the tiny forces that hold atoms together, to the huge forces that keep the planets traveling around the Sun, forces really are everywhere!

Some of the activities need patience—glue takes time to set, and adjustments may be needed to get something to work well. You don't have to do the experiments in order, although they make a little more sense if you do. The more you try out, the more you will discover about forces and motion—and the more fun you will have!

Stuck for words?

If you come across a word you don't know, or you just want to find out a little more, look in the glossary or the websites section on pages 30 and 31.

Clock symbol

The clock symbol at the start of each experiment shows you approximately how many minutes the activity should take. All take between 5 and 30 minutes. If you are using glue, allow extra time for drying.

Warning

Read through all the steps for an activity before you start. Then work through them steadily— rushing or getting carried away could cause an accident. A pair of scissors or a hammer could cause serious injury.

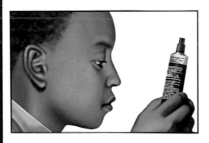

Ask an adult for help. Take special care when using glue. Make sure that you are using the right kind. Follow the instructions carefully and pay attention to any safety warnings. If in doubt, ask an adult. Have fun, but work safely!

Out of doors, stay away from traffic, open water, overhead power lines, or other hazards. Make sure a responsible adult knows where you are and what you are doing.

5

Measuring forces

Forces are all around us. They are the pushes and pulls that affect an object's shape and movement. A force's strength is measured in newtons (N), named after the English scientist Sir Isaac Newton. On Earth, everything has weight. This is the force of gravity pulling things down. Most people weigh things using pounds (lb.) or kilograms (kg). But because weight is a force, it should be measured in newtons. On Earth, a 3.5-oz. (100-g) mass weighs 1N.

You will need:

- A large yogurt tub or other plastic container
- String
- Two big paper clips
- A long, strong rubber band
- Paper, a marker, and a ruler
- A few full food packages with their mass in ounces on their labels
- A skewer

You will need:

- Two deep, empty cake pans, one smaller than the other
- A large spring from an old mattress or chair or a large sponge
- A 5-lb. bag of sugar
- A washable marker

Make a weighing scale

Put the spring or sponge into the big cake pan and then place the smaller pan on top. Put the bag of sugar into the smaller tin. Mark the "10N" level on the small pan, to align with the rim of the bigger pan. Use other heavy things to make a scale. You could use a kitchen scale to help you do this—remember 1 lb. weighs 4.5N.

What's going on?

In this experiment, the force of gravity is squashing a spring. The more mass an object has, the more strongly gravity pulls down on it, and the more the spring gets squashed.

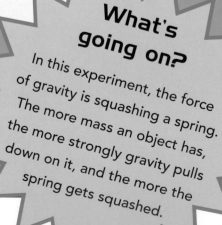

Make a force meter

It is easy to make a force meter, which you can use to measure the force of gravity.

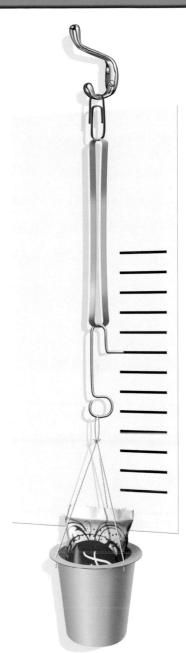

1 Find a hook somewhere and then attach a piece of paper to the wall below it. Loop the rubber band into a paper clip and hang the clip from the hook.

2 Open the other paper clip to make a hook at one end and a pointer at the other. You may need some help and a pair of pliers.

What's going on?

Things have weight because gravity pulls on them. The stronger the pull of gravity is on an object, the more it weighs. Weight is really the force of gravity acting on something. The force meter works because the heavier something is, the farther it stretches the rubber band.

3 Push holes around the rim of the tub. Use string to make a handle. Hang the tub from the rubber band with the bent paper clip.

4 Put the packages in the tub one at a time. Mark the position of the pointer each time and write the weight next to it to make a scale. Keep your eye level with the pointer. Do not overload the tub, or the rubber band will snap. To turn your scale into newtons, divide each weight in ounces by 3.5. For example, a 7-oz. package has a weight of 2N.

Squeezing and twisting

Forces can make things change shape. Whenever something is bent, twisted, squashed, or stretched, a force is acting on it. Springy or elastic materials try to go back to their original shape when the controlling force is removed. Thus, they can store up energy and then release it to make things move. Wind-up toys and some watches work like this.

What's going on?

You store up energy, known as potential energy, when you twist the rubber band. When you stop, the band unwinds and the longer toothpick leg turns and pushes the reel. The energy in the band becomes movement energy.

Wind-up toy

This intriguing toy shows how the energy stored in a twisted rubber band can cause movement. Use a couple of toothpicks.

1 Cut a thin slice from the wick end of the candle. Make the hole in the middle of the slice (where the wick was) big enough for the rubber band to fit through. Cut a groove in one side.

2 Poke the rubber band through the hole. Put a toothpick through the loop and pull on the other end of the rubber band so the toothpick fits into the groove. Thread the long end of the rubber band through the spool.

3 Push half a toothpick through the loop of rubber band you have just pulled through. Stop it from turning, either with tape or by wedging it with another half toothpick pushed into one of the holes in the spool.

You will need:

- A spool of thread
- A small rubber band
- Toothpicks
- Tape
- A candle
- A knife
- A skewer

Spring launcher

Attach the stick to the edge of a table with a blob of modeling clay. Slide the spiral, and then the spool, onto the stick. Press the spool down on the spiral and let go. How far does it fly? What happens if you give the spool more mass by sticking modeling clay to it?

What's going on?

The squashed spring pushes the spool, making it fly off the stick. The more mass the spool has, the greater the force required to make it fly the same distance.

4 Wind up your toy by holding the spool and turning the long toothpick around and round. Put it down on a flat surface and watch it crawl along!

You will need:

- A wire spiral from an old notebook
- A spool
- A thin, straight stick or rod
- Modeling clay

Explaining gravity

Everything is attracted to everything else by the force of gravity. The attraction between everyday things is too weak to notice. We only feel gravity pulling things down toward the ground so strongly because Earth has a lot of mass. The more mass something has, the stronger its gravitational pull. The Moon has less mass, so gravity is weaker there. Nobody is exactly sure what causes gravity, but without it we would all go flying off into space!

You will need:
- Cardboard
- Two semicircles of thin cardboard
- A ruler and pencil
- Tape
- Scissors

Antigravity

You would normally expect things to roll downhill. Or would you?

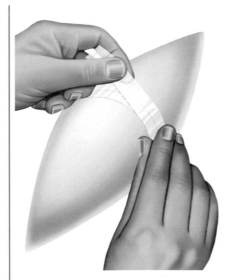

1 Cut two pieces of cardboard into the shape shown. Tape the shortest sides together. Position the two pieces as shown above.

2 Roll and stick the semicircles to make two matching cones. Tape the open ends together, as shown in the picture above.

What's going on?

The cones are not really defying gravity. They are actually going downhill. Watch the middle part carefully. Try measuring the distance from the middle of the cones to the ground at each end of the hill.

Do heavy things fall faster than light ones?

Find something safe to stand on (a sturdy chair will do), from which to drop your pairs of objects. Put the trays on the floor, one on each side of you. Drop both things from the same height at exactly the same time. Listen for them hitting the trays. Which one lands first? Try repeating your experiment to see if you get the same result every time.

You will need:

- Pairs of things that are the same size and shape—for example: a marble and a ball bearing; a dice and a sugar cube; a golf ball and a Ping-Pong ball
- Two cake pan lids or baking trays

What's going on?

Each pair should land together. Gravity makes them fall toward Earth at the same rate, even though they weigh different amounts. This is hard to believe until you see it for yourself!

3 Put the cones at the bottom of the hill and watch them appear to defy gravity by rolling uphill!

Balancing act

Something doesn't have to be moving to have a force acting on it. Gravity is pulling on you now, even if you are sitting still. So what makes things fall over? Every object has a center of gravity. This is the balancing point where the whole weight of the object seems to act. It affects how stable the object is. Things with a low center of gravity are very stable. Things with a high center of gravity tend to fall over.

What's going on?

A lot of the parrot's mass is in its huge tail. This gives it a low center gravity (actually below its feet), so it very stable and swings back upright ev when it is pushed over a little. You can get the same result if you make the tail smaller, then tape a coin to each side of it to give it more mass.

The perching parrot

This parrot will stay on its perch, even when you try to tip it over!

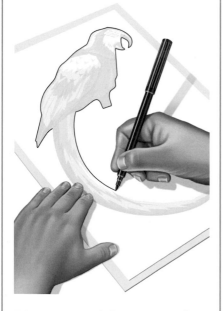

1 Trace around the picture of the parrot.

2 Transfer the outline to a piece of thick cardboard and cut it out.

3 Color in your parrot. Perch it on the edge of a table or on a taut piece of string.

You will need:

- Thick cardboard
- Tracing paper
- A pencil
- Coins
- Felt-tip pens
- Scissors
- A table or some string

Magic box

Tape the weight into a corner of the box and put the lid on it. Slide the box over the edge of a table until only the corner with the weight in it is on the table. The rest of the box seems to be held up by thin air! If you make a false bottom to hide the weight, you can even take the lid off to show that the box is "empty!"

You will need:

- A small box
- A heavy weight or several coins stuck together
- Tape

What's going on?

A box is a regular shape, so you would expect its center of gravity to be in the middle. Adding the weight moves the center of gravity toward the corner. As long as the box's center of gravity is above the table, the box will not fall off.

Under pressure

You can't push your thumb into a cork. But you can easily push a thumbtack into a cork using the same force. This is because the point of the thumbtack concentrates the force on to a tiny area, causing a lot of pressure. The pressure on your thumb is much lower, because the same force is spread out over the thumbtack's big, flat head. The more a force is spread out, the lower the pressure is.

Air pressure

The force of the air pressing on things is called air pressure. Although you can't see air pressure, you can see its effect with this quick experiment.

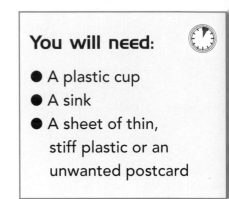

You will need:

- A plastic cup
- A sink
- A sheet of thin, stiff plastic or an unwanted postcard

1 Fill the cup right up to the brim with water and slide the postcard over the top.

2 Hold the postcard against the cup with one hand. Hold onto the cup with your other hand.

3 Holding the postcard in place, turn the cup upside down over the sink. Let go of the postcard. It should stay put, held up by nothing but air pressure!

Spread the force

Try pressing a coin into a lump of modeling clay with the flat side down. Then try pressing it in with the edge down. Which is easier?

You will need:

- A coin
- Modeling clay

What's going on?

The edge of the coin is much easier to push in. The smaller the area, the bigger the pressure of your hand's force. The coin's face has a much bigger area so it spreads the force, causing a lower pressure.

What's going on?

Air pressure pushes in all directions, including upward. It is easily strong enough to hold up the weight of water in a cup. The postcard acts as a seal, keeping air out of the cup as you turn it upside down. In fact, air is pressing in on every square inch of your body with a force of about 15 lb., or 67.5N. You are not crushed because your body is pushing back with an equal, opposite force.

Floating and sinking

Whether something floats or sinks depends on its density. This is a way of measuring how heavy something is for its size. A steel cube, for instance, is a lot heavier than a cube of ice of the same size. The steel cube will sink in water, but the ice cube floats. We say that ice is less dense than water—in other words, a cube of ice weighs less than a cube of water the same size. So far so good, but how can a steel ship stay afloat?

Deep-sea diver

You can see how changing something's density makes it float or sink by making this model of a diver.

I Cut out the shape of your diver from the pie plate. Make him tall and thin, about 2¹/₂ in. (7cm) by ³/₄ in. (2cm), so he will fit through the neck of the bottle!

2 Bend the straw at the neck and then cut it so you have a U-shaped piece about 1 in. (2.5cm) long. Slide the open ends of the straw onto the two ends of the paper clip.

3 Slide the paper clip and straw between the diver's legs and up onto his body. The straw should be on his back, bent at the top behind his head.

4 Make diving boots out of modeling clay and put them on his feet.

5 Try floating your diver in a bowl of water. Carefully adjust the amount of modeling clay on his boots until he just floats.

6 Fill the bottle with water and put the diver inside. Make sure the bottle is full to the top and then screw the cap on tightly. The diver should float to the top.

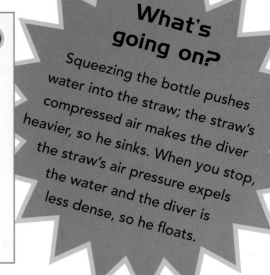

What's going on?

Squeezing the bottle pushes water into the straw; the straw's compressed air makes the diver heavier, so he sinks. When you stop, the straw's air pressure expels the water and the diver is less dense, so he floats.

7 Squeeze the bottle. The diver will sink to the bottom. Let go, and he'll float up. With care, you can make him float as deep as you like!

How does a boat float?

Test your objects to see which ones float and which sink. Drop a ball of modeling clay into the water. Flatten it out and make it into a bowl shape. Will it float now? Try the same with aluminum foil.

What's going on?

Small, heavy things sink; large, light things float. But if you make a hollow bowl shape out of something small and heavy such as clay, most of the bowl is filled with air. The bowl and air are less dense than water, so the bowl floats.

Faster and faster

Forces can make things speed up, or accelerate. If the forces on something are balanced, it won't change speed. But if the force pushing an object forward is greater than the force pushing it back, it will get faster and faster until the forces are in balance. Unbalanced forces can make things change speed or direction.

What's going on?

The boat is powered by the energy stored in the rubber band when you wind it up. As the paddle turns, it pushes against the water, unbalancing the forces on the bottle. It accelerates until the resistance of the water pushing back is equal to the force of the paddle pushing forward, and the forces are balanced. Then it continues at a steady speed until the rubber band runs out of stored energy.

Paddle boat

This little paddle boat shows how unbalanced forces can push something forward.

You will need:

- A two-liter plastic bottle
- Two sticks about 9 in. (23cm) long
- A plastic container with flat sides
- Scissors
- Waterproof tape
- A rubber band, about 3.5 in. (9cm) long

1 Cut four rectangles from the flat sides of the plastic container, 2 in. (5cm) by 3 in. (8cm) each.

2 Fold the rectangles in half and stand them on their long sides. Bring the folded edges together and secure them with tape to make a paddle.

3 Tape the two sticks to opposite sides of the bottle about three-quarters of the way down, so they stick out by about 3 in. (7cm).

Balloon boat

Soften the balloon by blowing it up a couple of times. Tape it to the straw and check that the seal is airtight. Make a small hole in one end of the tray, big enough for the straw to go through. Put the straw through the hole, blow up the balloon, and seal the end of the straw with modeling clay. Put the boat in some water and snip off the modeling clay.

You will need:

- Plastic tray (the kind microwave meals come in)
- A flexible straw
- Modeling clay
- A balloon
- Tape and scissors

What's going on?

The balloon pushes air out through the straw, which pushes the boat forward. Jet engines and rockets work in just the same way, except they are pushed forward by gases shooting out at the back.

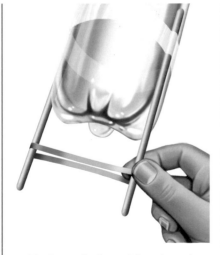

4 Stretch the rubber band over the sticks. Use one that fits easily without being tightly stretched.

5 Slide the paddle inside the rubber band and wind it up. Put your boat in a bath or pool of water and let go!

Measuring up

Measuring speed can be very useful. Car drivers, for example, need to know if they are staying below the speed limit. Train drivers need to know if they are going at the right speed to get to the next station at the right time. To figure out how fast something is going, you need to know two things—the distance it has traveled and the time it has taken to do it.

What's going on?

Average speed tells you how far the cyclist goes each second. For example, if the cyclist goes 100 ft. (30m) in 5 seconds, her average speed is 100/5, which is 20 ft. per second, or 20 ft./s. Speed is often measured in miles per hour (mph) or kilometers per hour (km/h), but the idea is the same.

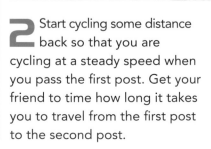

Speed trial

Here is an easy way to measure how fast a cyclist is going. Ask an adult to find you a safe, traffic-free cycle path for this experiment.

You will need:

- A bicycle
- A stopwatch or a watch with a second hand
- A measuring tape
- A calculator
- A friend

1 Measure the distance between two things along the side of the path (trees, for example). Try to choose things about 100 ft. (30m) apart.

2 Start cycling some distance back so that you are cycling at a steady speed when you pass the first post. Get your friend to time how long it takes you to travel from the first post to the second post.

Balloon rocket

Cut a few straws into 4-in. (10-cm) lengths. Thread them onto the end of the string. Tie the string between two chairs about 30 ft. (10m) apart and pull it tight. Blow up a balloon. Keep the neck tightly pinched and ask your friend to tape it to the first piece of straw and then let it go! With your watch, time how long the balloon takes to fly to the far end of the string. See which shaped balloons go the fastest.

You will need:

- A pack of balloons
- Drinking straws
- Tape
- A ball of string
- A measuring tape
- A stopwatch
- A friend

$$\text{Average speed} = \frac{\text{Distance traveled}}{\text{Time taken}}$$

3 Use this equation to figure out how fast you were going. If you measure the distance in feet and time in seconds, the answer will be in feet per second, or ft./s. for short.

What's going on?

The deflating balloon squeezes the air inside, forcing it out of the end. This pushes the balloon forward. Long, thin balloons fly faster than round ones because they are more streamlined and have to push less air out of the way as they go forward.

Friction—the invisible force

Whenever things rub together, friction is produced. It is an invisible force that can stop movement. Friction also happens when something moves through a fluid, such as water, or through a gas, such as air. Then it is often called "drag." Sometimes friction is useful when it provides grip or slows something down, but it can be a nuisance. On your bicycle, you can oil moving parts such as the chain to reduce friction, but you would never put oil on the wheel rims where the brake pads rub!

You will need:

- A large wooden board
- A smooth plastic tray
- An assortment of flat-bottomed objects that won't break easily —for example, a plastic cup, coin, rubber, or a matchbox

Slide or grip?

This quick experiment shows how the amount of friction between two surfaces depends on how rough or smooth they are.

1 Line up your objects along one end of the wooden board. Predict which one you think will slide the most easily.

2 Slowly lift the end of the board and find out which thing slips the most easily and which is the stickiest.

3 Now try using the plastic tray. How much difference does it make?

What's going on?

Some things slide along the wooden board more easily than others because there is less friction between their bottom surface and the board. They will probably be the objects that feel smoother to the touch. Things slide much more easily along a smooth surface, such as the plastic tray, for the same reason.

Rubbing hands

Rub together the palms of your hands, at first quite gently and slowly, then harder and quicker. What do you notice? Make them wet and soapy and then try the same thing again.

You will need:
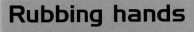

- Your hands!
- Soap and water

What's going on?

The harder you press your hands together and the faster you rub, the hotter they feel. This is because rubbing your hands produces friction, and friction causes heat. When you do the same thing with wet, soapy hands, the soapy water reduces the friction and so your hands feel less hot.

Force magnifiers

Levers and pulleys are "force magnifiers." How would you get the lid off a can of paint? You could use a screwdriver as a lever. Think about a door handle. You push the handle a long way to make the latch move only a little to open the door. These are "force magnifiers." A small force is used to move one end a long way, causing a big force to move something a short distance at the other end.

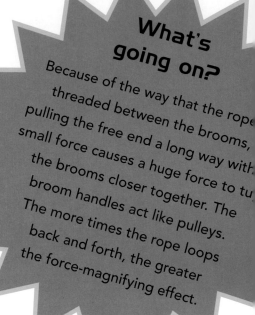

What's going on?

Because of the way that the rope threaded between the brooms, pulling the free end a long way with small force causes a huge force to tu the brooms closer together. The broom handles act like pulleys. The more times the rope loops back and forth, the greater the force-magnifying effect.

You will need:

- Two brooms or mops
- Several feet of rope
- Some talcum powder
- A few friends

Pulley power

Delight your friends and worry your enemies with this demonstration of your super-human strength!

1 Tie the rope near the end of one broom.

2 Dust the two broom handles with talcum powder to reduce friction.

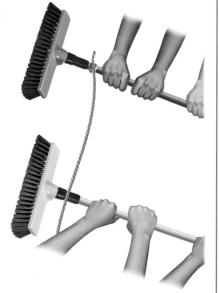

3 Get two or even four friends to hold the two brooms far apart from each other.

Levers

Ask an adult to bang the lid onto the tin really tightly. Try levering it off, first with the handle of a teaspoon and then with the dessert spoon handle. Be careful not to bend the spoons or make a mess! Which spoon works best?

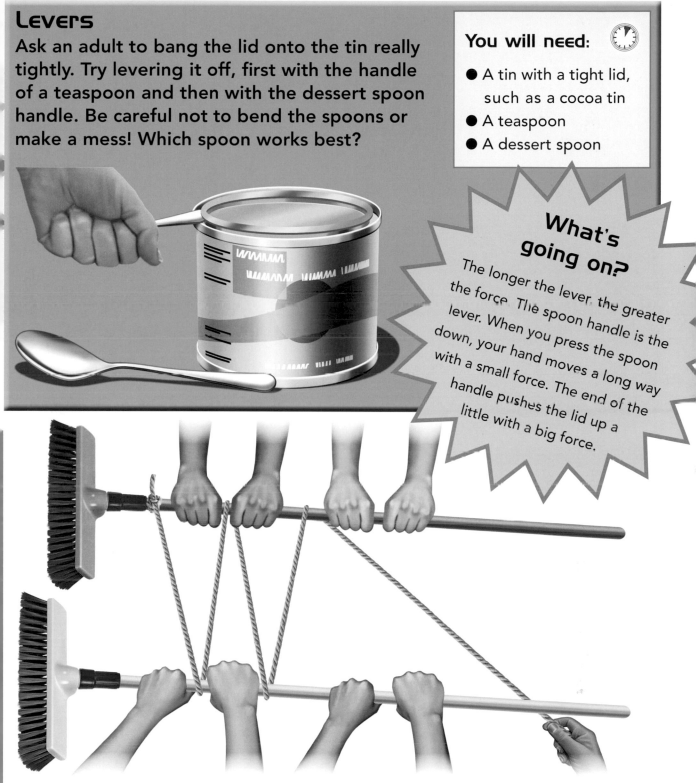

What's going on?

The longer the lever, the greater the force. The spoon handle is the lever. When you press the spoon down, your hand moves a long way with a small force. The end of the handle pushes the lid up a little with a big force.

4 Thread the rope around the two brooms as shown. Grab hold of the free end of the rope.

Tell your friends to try and keep the brooms apart with all their strength while you effortlessly,

with your super powers, pull them together!

Gears—wheels with teeth

Gears are wheels with teeth around the outside. They can be connected directly together or joined by a chain. Depending on the sizes of the gear wheels, gears can be used as force magnifiers or as movement magnifiers. They are used in all sorts of machines to change the speed or direction of movement. Bicycles and cars need gears to cope with going up and down hills and traveling at various speeds.

What's going on?

A low gear works as a force magnifier. It is very slow on flat gro__ but good for climbing hills. The ped__ go around quickly compared to the wh__ The high gear is for pedaling downhi__ or going fast on the level. The wheel goes around quickly compared to the pedals, but with much less power.

Bicycle gears

This experiment will show you the effect that gears have on a bicycle's movement.

You will need:

- A bicycle with gears
- A tape measure
- Some chalk
- A quiet, level path away from any traffic

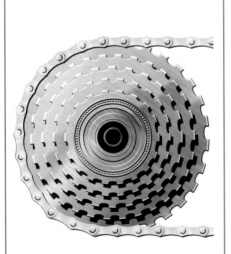

1 Put the bicycle into its lowest gear.

2 Make a chalk mark on the path beside the back wheel, where it touches the ground.

3 Gently turn the pedals once, walking the bicycle forward in a straight line.

Making gears

Mark the center of each lid and ask an adult to punch a hole through them. Glue a spool on to each lid in line with the hole. Stretch a thick rubber band around the rim of each lid to give them grip. Push two nails through the cardboard, spaced apart so that when you slot two lids over them, their rims just touch. Turn the larger lid and see how the smaller lid moves. Try some different lid size combinations.

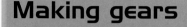

You will need:

- Jar lids of various sizes
- Wide rubber bands
- Thick cardboard
- A hammer
- Two 1½-in. (4-cm) nails
- Spools

What's going on?

This is just like the top gear on a bike, only without the chain to link the two wheels. Turning the large wheel slowly makes the small wheel spin quickly, in the opposite direction. To change into bottom gear, use the small wheel to turn the big one. The big wheel will turn slowly with some force.

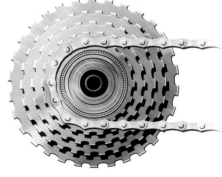

Make a second mark next to the back wheel. Measure the distance between the marks.

4 Put the bicycle into top gear and repeat the experiment. How far does it go this time?

Circular motion

Anything spinning around has circular motion. Moving things will always go in a straight line unless there is a force tugging them off course. When something moves in a circle, it is constantly changing direction. For this to happen, there has to be a force pulling it toward the middle of the circle. This is centripetal force. You can easily feel this force on a playground merry-go-round, tugging on your arms as your body tries to fly off in a straight line!

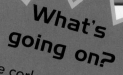

What's going on?

As the cork spins faster, the centripetal force needed to keep it going around in a circle, instead flying off in a straight line, increases. This force tugs on the string, lifting up the weight. The faster you spin the cork, the higher the weight is lifted until it reaches the spool.

Spinning force

This experiment shows how centripetal force increases, the faster something spins around. Find a space away from other people in which to do this!

You will need:

- A cork or rubber bung
- About 3 ft. (1m) of string
- A spool
- A small weight, such as a wooden block
- A drill (ask an adult)

1 Ask an adult to drill a small hole lengthwise through the cork.

2 Thread one end of the string through the cork and tie a knot in the end, big enough to stop the cork from sliding off.

3 Thread the other end of the string through the spool and tie it to the weight.

Make a spinner

Draw a circle on the cardboard and cut it out. Carefully push the pointed end of a pencil through the center of the circle. Spin the pencil on a smooth, flat surface. What happens if the cardboard is low down on the pencil?

You will need:

- A compass
- Cardboard or thin, stiff plastic
- Scissors
- A pencil

What's going on?

Spinning objects, such as wheels, resist being tilted. This makes them stable. The spinner balances the pencil, especially when the center of gravity is kept low by having the cardboard low down on the pencil.

4 Hold the spool. Start whirling the cork around in a circle, slowly at first and then faster and faster.

Glossary

ACCELERATION When an object increases its speed, it is accelerating. Acceleration is measured in feet per second squared (ft./s.^{2}).

AIR PRESSURE The pressure caused by the weight of Earth's atmosphere, also called atmospheric pressure. Although it is invisible, air has mass, so it is pulled down by Earth's gravity. The pressure of the air at Earth's surface is about 67.5 newtons per square inch, or 10N per square centimeter. Weather maps show areas of higher or lower air pressure, as these have a strong effect on the weather.

BALANCED FORCES Forces that do not cause any change in the motion of an object, when they interact, are said to be balanced. When you sit on a chair, for example, the force of gravity pulling you down is balanced by the equal and opposite reaction force of the chair pushing you up.

CENTER OF GRAVITY
(or center of mass) The point in an object where the force of gravity appears to act. If it is suspended from any point on the vertical line passing through its center of gravity, the object will stay balanced.

CENTRIPETAL FORCE
The force that causes something to move in a circular path. When you twirl a stone around on a string, you have to pull on the string to keep the stone from flying off in a straight line. The force of the string tugging on the stone is the centripetal force.

DENSITY How much mass something has in relation to its volume. Density is a substance's mass divided by its volume, measured in grams per centimeter cubed (g/cm^3).

DRAG An aerodynamic force that resists the forward motion of an object. The shape of the object affects the amount of drag.

ENERGY The ability to do work. Work is done whenever a force moves through a distance, so you can think of energy as a "promise" to do work. There are several kinds of energy, such as light, heat, electrical energy, and potential energy. Both work and energy are measured in joules (J).

FORCE MAGNIFIER
A machine where a small force moving a long distance causes a big force to move a small distance—for example, a door handle opening a door.

FORCES The pushes or pulls that can change something's speed, shape, or direction. Forces are measured in newtons (N).

FRICTION The rubbing force that resists movement when things slide against each other.

GEARS Toothed wheels used in machines to make one wheel turn another.

GRAVITATIONAL PULL
The pull of one object on another due to the force of gravity. For example, Earth's gravity keeps satellites traveling in orbit around the planet.

GRAVITY A force of attraction that pulls everything toward everything else. The strength of attraction depends on the mass of the objects and how far apart they are.

INERTIA The tendency of any object to stay still or move steadily in a straight line unless a force makes it do otherwise. The more mass something has, the greater its inertia.

KILOGRAM (kg) The standard unit of mass used in science. A volume of one liter of water has a mass of one kilogram.

LEVER A rigid bar that can turn on a pivot or hinge to transmit a force from one place to another. Wheelbarrows, scissors, and the body's muscles and joints are all examples of lever systems.

MACHINE A device that does work. Machines are designed to make life easier for us.

MASS The amount of material that an object contains.

MOTION Motion occurs when something changes its position.

MOVEMENT MAGNIFIER
A mechanism where a large force moving a short distance causes a small force to move a long distance—for example, the pedal that opens the lid of a garbage can.

NEWTON (N) Unit for measuring forces. The pull of Earth's gravity on a mass of $3\frac{1}{2}$ oz. (100g) is almost exactly 1N.

POTENTIAL ENERGY Stored energy. When you lift something or pull a spring, you give it potential energy.

PRESSURE How concentrated or spread out a force is over a surface. Pressure is calculated by dividing the size of the force by the area it is acting on. It is measured in pascals (Pa) or newtons per square meter (N/m^2).

PULLEY A wheel with a grooved rim. Several can be used together to make it easier to lift a heavy load. This is an example of a force magnifier.

SPEED How fast something is going. Speed is calculated by dividing distance by time. Average speed is the total distance traveled on a journey divided by the total time taken.

STREAMLINED A shape that encounters less friction and reduces drag. A fish has a streamlined shape.

TURNING FORCE The strength of a turning effect. The longer a lever, the greater the turning force it can produce.

UNBALANCED FORCES Forces that cause a change in the motion or shape of an object, because the force acting in one direction is greater than the force acting in the opposite direction.

UPTHRUST The upward force that acts on an object when it is immersed in a fluid. The size of the force is the same as the weight of the fluid that makes way for the object.

WEIGHT A measurement of the force of gravity pulling on a mass on or near the surface of the planet.

Websites

If you have enjoyed this book, the websites below will give you even more information on forces and motion. Many of them have fun games to play that will help you understand the difficult sections.

Forces:
- www.bbc.co.uk/schools/ks2bitesize/science/ physical_processes/forces_action/read1.shtml
- www.engineeringinteract.org
- http://primaryhomeworkhelp.co.uk/revision/Science/ physical.htm

Motion:
- www.physics4kids.com/files/motion_intro.html
- www.channel4learning.com/apps26/learning/ microsites/E/essentials/science/physical/friction_ bi.jsp

Index

A B C
balancing 12, 13
bicycles 20, 26, 27
boats 17, 18, 19

D
density 16, 17
divers 16, 17
drag 19, 22

E F
elastic 8
energy
  movement 8
  potential 8, 9, 18
floating 16, 17
forces
  balanced 18
  centripetal 28, 29
  force magnifiers 24, 25, 26
  force meter 6
  friction 22, 23, 24
  measuring of 6
  newtons 6, 7
  unbalanced 18
  weight 6

G H
gears 26, 27
gravity
  center of 12, 13, 29
  force of 6, 7, 10, 11, 29

I J K
kilograms 6

L
levers 25

M N O
mass 7, 9, 10, 12, 13
Moon 7, 10, 11
motion
  acceleration 18, 19
  average speed 20, 21
  circular 28, 29
  magnifiers 26
  measuring speed 20, 21
  movement
Newton, Isaac 6

P
pounds 6
pressure 14, 15, 23
pulleys 24, 25

Q R
resistance
  water 18

S
spinners 29
streamlining 21, 27

W X Y Z
weighing scales 7

32